OF TRAINING AND SPIRITUAL GROWTH

In my thirty-six years with the airline it seemed that I never stopped training. There was initial training (when I first hired on to fly). There was recurrent training (at least once a year and often twice a year I went to ground school and flight-simulator training). If I changed airplanes, I received transition training (equipping me to fly that particular kind of airplane). All of this training was for the purpose of providing me with knowledge, checking my knowledge, and reinforcing my knowledge to fly safely and to handle any emergencies that might arise.

One thing was sure: my life with the airline was neither stagnant nor routine—always changing and challenging, always equipping me to grow in proficiency and professionalism.

While some flight crews complained about all the training, I looked forward to it. It sharpened my skills, increased my comfort level with the aircraft, and gave me confidence.

In a similar way, our walk with the Lord involves growing, exercising our spiritual knowledge, learning, testing, and training.

> "But grow in grace, and in the knowledge of our Lord and Saviour Jesus Christ" (2 Peter 3:18, KJV).

Christian growth should not be stagnant. Scripture speaks of our new birth by faith in Christ as our Savior. It also speaks of our spiritual growth:

> "Like newborn babies, long for the pure milk of the word, so that by it you may grow in respect to salvation" (1 Peter 2:2, NASB).

Babies should grow both physically and mentally. Likewise, Christians should grow. But how do we grow in the grace and knowledge of Christ? The Word of God is "milk and meat" to the new believer. Reading, studying, and hearing the preaching and teaching of God's Word strengthens us spiritually. As believers, we learn how to live, how not to live, how to serve God, and how to discern truth and error. All of this helps us to grow in grace.

Our airline training involved time, directed study, repetition, and review of facts. The training helped us to grow from novices to professionals. Christian maturity (learning and moving forward in our walk with God) is both needful and necessary. No one should remain a spiritual baby, simply feeding on "milk" due to being sluggish about his or her spiritual growth. (See Hebrews 5:11, *Amplified Bible*.)

People who are growing spiritually spend time in the Word of God and apply the Scriptures in their life experiences to help them discern between good and evil and to follow God's will in purpose, thought, and action.

> "But solid food is for the mature, for those who have their powers of discernment trained by constant practice to distinguish good from evil" (Hebrews 5:14, ESV).

Most of our airline training was in a classroom. Where is God's classroom for Christian training? It is best found in a Bible-teaching and Scripture-preaching local church.

> Hebrews 10:25 (NKJV) states: "Not forsaking the assembling of ourselves together, as is the manner of some, but exhorting one another, and so much the more as you see the day approaching."

So as we used to say in the airline, "I'll see you in training!"

THE JOY OF GIVING

I had the blessing of wonderful Christian parents who taught me early on the privilege of giving to God. With a weekly allowance of one dollar, I would receive ten dimes from my dad. He would say, "Put one dime in the offering at church." Later, when I trusted Christ as my personal Savior, Christian giving was already a habit in my life.

Airline flying was a lucrative profession. As my income increased, my late wife and I joyfully increased the percentage of our giving to the Lord. Even though our income was steady, there were uncertain times. For example, during the fuel crisis of the 1970s, I was faced with a possible layoff (called a "furlough" within the industry). We decided that we would just keep giving. Thankfully, the furlough was cancelled.

Later in my career, the pilots (along with all employees) were asked to take pay cuts to help the airline. This we did. And once again, we just kept giving.

Thankfully, the pay cuts ended, and we were returned to our previous salaries.

About six months before my mandatory retirement at age sixty, my pilot pension was terminated by the bankruptcy court to help bring the airline out of bankruptcy. I had no idea just what my retirement income would be—if anything at all. However, we just kept giving, and God just kept supplying our needs, just as He promised in Philippians 4:19 (NASB): "And my God will supply all your needs according to His riches in glory in Christ Jesus."

God also promises to supply the gift and bless the giver: "And God is able to make all grace abound to you, so that always having all sufficiency in everything, you may have an abundance for every good deed" (2 Corinthians 9:8, NASB—for further reading on this, read 2 Corinthians chapters 8 and 9).

Do we give in order to get from God? No. Do we give to get a tax deduction? No. We should give from grateful hearts, because He gave His Son to die for our sins and "gives us richly all things to enjoy" (1 Timothy 6:17, NKJV).

THIS IS YOUR CAPTAIN SPEAKING

Public address announcements from the cockpit to the passenger cabin are both frequent and required in airline flying. As Brenda often says, "Informed people are happy people." This is especially true when flights are delayed, diverted, or out of the normal routine. As a pilot, my practice was to make PAs true, simple, and clear. If the flight was delayed, I would apologize and would stress what we were doing to get back on schedule. Naturally, I expressed gratitude to the passengers for choosing to fly with us.

Think about God's special announcements, as recorded in the Bible. For example: God told Adam the new conditions under which he must live, because he had sinned against God; His promise to Noah at the ark; God's plan for Moses as revealed at the burning bush; His commission of Joshua to lead His people. In the New Testament, God made special announcements to Joseph and Mary; to the shepherds, regarding Christ's birth; and to John, regarding Christ's return.

Do we have any "announcements" from God today? Yes! It is His complete love letter to us via His Word, the Bible.

> Second Peter 1:3–4 (NKJV) states: "As His divine power has given to us all things that pertain to life and godliness, through the knowledge of Him who called us by glory and virtue, by which have been given to us exceedingly great and precious promises, that through these you may be partakers of the divine nature, having escaped the corruption that is in the world through lust."

Proverbs 22:20 (KJV) further reminds us that He has: "written to thee excellent things in counsels and knowledge."

Therefore, we can ask God to open our eyes, "so that [we] may behold wondrous things out of [His] law" (Psalm 119:18, KJV).

STAY ON COURSE

The last five years during my career as an airline pilot, I flew back and forth from Philadelphia to seven cities in Europe. International flying across the North Atlantic brought a different set of procedures and practices that were required to operate the plane safely and efficiently. It was critical that both the assigned navigation route and the course were maintained. This was accomplished through on-board computerized guidance systems. However, these systems were cross-checked every thirty to forty-five minutes by the cockpit crew to make sure that the plane was where it should be!

Similarly, God has not left us without His help. Look at Psalm 119:105 (NKJV): "Your word is a lamp to my feet and a light to my path."

We need guidance for everyday living as well as future guidance for the path ahead. God has promised to instruct us in the way we should go (see Psalm 32:8).

Just as the crew in the cockpit continuously cross-checks the plane's location in order to stay on course, you can go daily to God's Word for His guidance as you seek His will for your life.

WATCHING THE AIR SPACE

Throughout my career with the airlines, I had many radio communications with the men and women of the air traffic control service. Each day these passionate professionals control thousands of flights with one goal: keeping two airplanes from being in the same air space at the same time!

While the airline crew plans the flight's route, altitude, and air speed, the air traffic controller accepts the flight plan into the big picture on his or her radar scope, which includes all the other flights operating within that air space. The air traffic controller has the authority to change the plane's route, altitude, and air speed in order to separate the traffic of the multiple airplanes within that space.

Just as each person is a unique individual, each flight is assigned a four-digit code, which is entered into the on-board electronic equipment, and that sends a unique symbol next to that plane on the radar scope. This gives the controller continuous, positive identification of the plane, including its altitude, speed, and destination. The air traffic controller is always watching his or her assigned flight(s).

In a similar way, our wonderful God is always watching over us and is aware of our situation. Even before our birth, God knew all about us:

> "For You formed my inward parts; You covered me in my mother's womb. I will praise You, for I am fearfully and wonderfully made; marvelous are Your works, and that my soul knows very well. My frame was not hidden from You, when I was made in secret, and skillfully wrought in the lowest parts of the earth. Your eyes saw my substance, being yet unformed. And in Your book they all were written, the days fashioned for me, when as yet there were none of them" (Psalm 139:13–16, NKJV).

God also knows the way (or direction) that our lives take:

> "But He knows the way that I take; when He has tested me, I shall come forth as gold" (Job 23:10, NKJV).

> "You comprehend my path and my lying down, and are acquainted with all my ways" (Psalm 139:3, NKJV).

Additionally, God guides us today, just as He guided Isaiah in the Old Testament:

"Your ears shall hear a word behind you, saying, 'This is the way, walk in it,' whenever you turn to the right hand or whenever you turn to the left" (Isaiah 30:21, NKJV).

Therefore, just as we and our entire flight crew trusted the air traffic controllers for a safe and clear air space, so also we as believers can trust a more infinitely wonderful God to watch over us and to guide our lives and our destiny.

"For this God is our God for ever and ever: he will be our guide even unto death" (Psalm 48:14, KJV).

CONTRAILS IN THE SKY

Recently, Brenda and I saw a spectacular display of contrails (short for "condensation trails"). Covering the winter-morning sky were several crisscrossing white vapor trails that extended great distances. (On the front cover of this book, you can see the actual picture we took that morning!)

These "fingers in the sky" are formed when the water vapor from the jet engine exhaust of airplanes at high altitudes instantly freezes. These thin streams of vapor sometimes can extend for miles behind the airplane.

On a smaller scale, think of the visible water vapor formed by your breath on a cold day or from a car exhaust in cold weather. It's a very similar concept.

As I saw these contrails, I was quickly reminded of God's Word describing life as "a vapor that appears for a little while and then vanishes away" (James 4:14, NASB).

Additionally, Proverbs 27:1 (NKJV) states: "Do not boast about tomorrow, for you do not know what a day may bring forth."

I encourage you today to take your focus off of that which "vanishes away." Instead, take a moment to pray the words of Psalm 90:12 (KJV): "So teach us to number our days, that we may apply our hearts unto wisdom."

THE NAVIGATIONAL COMPASS

Flying involves working with several areas of knowledge—for example, weather, the physics of flight, navigation, and federal air regulations. Perhaps my favorite of these is navigation, which is the art and science of drawing a line on a map, figuring wind direction and speed, and finding where to point the nose of the airplane in order to get from origin to destination.

All cockpits contain a compass. Yes, computers and global satellite positioning systems do the majority of the work, but if these should fail, the compass is there, ready to give direction and guidance for where you wish to go. The compass's alignment is governed by the magnetic field in God's masterfully created earth.

Indeed, Scripture declares that God "set a compass upon the face of the depth" (Proverbs 8:27, KJV). The security and sufficiency of the compass remind me of God's abiding presence.

Psalm 139:7–10 (NKJV) wonderfully declares that God is always there:

> "Where can I go from Your Spirit? Or where can I flee from Your presence? If I ascend into heaven, You are there; If I make my bed in hell, behold, You are there. If I take the wings of the morning, And dwell in the uttermost parts of the sea, even there Your hand shall lead me, And Your right hand shall hold me."

You can't hide from God.

You can't run from God.

He is near and available to guide you in the direction that you should go.

THE BEST SEAT IN THE HOUSE

Whether you fly as a pilot or as a passenger, the view from the airplane is not only beautiful; it is also fascinating. Throughout my flying career, such panoramas gripped my attention, and I loved every second of the show.

Ground patterns, colors, vistas, clouds, mountains, rivers, cities, fields, lakes, and oceans—all provided thrilling and unique visual displays. No flight was "routine." Even though the sights changed constantly, I never got tired of the scenery.

One sight was the seemingly continuous sunset as I flew westbound from the East Coast. Likewise, the morning star, ushering in the dawn of the day (after I had flown most of the night across the North Atlantic), would capture my attention and imagination. Clouds presented tantalizing shapes as they grew to a height that far exceeded our cruising altitude. Flying over a flat cloud layer would sometimes allow me to see "the pilot's glory"—a beautiful rainbow ring around the shadow of the airplane, reflecting on the cloud layer. Night flying provided the appearance of "jewels on black velvet," with the pinpoint appearance of lights from cities and towns sparkling upward from within the dark landscape. Moonlight, along with starlight, had a distinct beauty.

I gratefully observed all of this from what pilots often call "the best seat in the house": the pilot's seat. The psalmist, in Psalm 19:1 (KJV), gives credit to God for the beauty of His creation: "The heavens declare the glory of God; and the firmament sheweth his handywork."

Psalm 104:24 (NKJV) speaks of the magnitude of the scope of this creation: "O Lord, how manifold are Your works! In wisdom You have made them all. The earth is full of Your possessions."

Don't wait until your next flight to observe this creation and to praise the Creator! Praise Him now! He is worthy!

READING, GROWING, LEARNING

Recently my wife and I were at an antique store, indulging in one of our favorite pastimes: rummaging through antique stores and their contents. My eyes were fixed quickly on a soft-bound aviation textbook. It was familiar to me, because it was the first of several aviation texts that I would read and study. It contained the Federal Aviation Regulations and included a very unique description (complete with cartoon-like characters) of various flight maneuvers that I would be learning and practicing in my flight training.

At the end of the book was a Solo Flight Certificate, which was later completed for me by my flight instructor on the day that I took off and landed all by my excited self. That certificate, dated over fifty years ago, now hangs in the office in our home.

When it comes to reading and the various subjects related to work within the airline industry (weather, theory of flight, navigation, and the Federal Air Regulations), I have concluded that pilots never quit reading or learning about flying. In addition to that first text book, I was later assigned reading that came in heavy, ring-bound books and that contained advanced information about the airplane, its various systems, and flight operations at the airline. There was so much that we had to read, learn, know, and remember!

God has given us His Word to guide us, equip us, and to help us live godly lives. But when I read the Bible, do I understand all that I read? No. Do I comprehend all that I read? No. However, I *believe* all that I read. That is why I have been reading God's Word regularly and systematically for quite some time.

Have a Bible-reading plan. Many are available on the Internet, and some Bibles even contain a reading schedule, which, if followed, will guide you through reading the Bible in its entirety within a given time frame.

As I mentioned previously, when I was in college, I began a Bible-reading plan that would take a year to finish. I would read two chapters of the Old Testament, two chapters of the New Testament, five Psalms, and one chapter from Proverbs.

In a thirty-day month, reading five Psalms a day, you can read the book of Psalms (a book of praise to God).

Choose a Bible translation that is reliable and readable. Then, begin reading! God's wonderful and sufficient Word, His love letter to us, will never cease to exist or go out of date. It is there to teach us how to live.

In 2 Timothy 3:16–17 (NASB), the Bible states: "All Scripture is inspired by God and profitable for teaching, for reproof, for correction, for training in righteousness; so that the man of God may be adequate, equipped for every good work."

Joe Henderson

CALLING OUT TO GOD

It was the second semester of my senior year of college, and I was struggling with organic chemistry. Someone from the dean's office called to ask why I hadn't registered for graduation. I didn't think I had enough credits. However, the caller stated that if I passed organic chemistry, I'd have enough credits to graduate!

At that same time, the airlines were hiring, and I needed a college degree to get the job. But first, I needed a grade of ninety-four percent or better on my second test out of three to pass this class. Be assured that I studied all night for that test, and that I studied diligently. I called out to the Lord to help me do my best and to pass that test. However, the test was hard, and I didn't finish it.

Three weeks later, the professor said, "Nobody finished the last test. So I'm going to give everyone a ninety-four percent—for averaging purposes—and not curve the grades the rest of the semester."

By the time the final exam rolled around, I had actually raised my grade by a full letter grade, and I passed the course!

One course. One test. One grade. My future career as a pilot hinged on this one pivotal moment.

I have since called this my "Jeremiah 33:3 experience!"

> "Call unto me, and I will answer thee, and show thee great and mighty things, which thou knowest not" (Jeremiah 33:3, KJV).

No, when we call on the Lord, He doesn't always give us a passing grade, a good medical report, the financial amount that we're lacking. But He does promise to answer us and show us "great and mighty things" through His answer!

SHARING THE GOSPEL

Before He ascended to heaven, our Lord Jesus Christ gave His disciples the Great Commission:

> "Go ye therefore, and teach all nations, baptizing them in the name of the Father, and of the Son, and of the Holy Ghost: Teaching them to observe all things whatsoever I have commanded you: and, lo, I am with you always, even unto the end of the world. Amen" (Matthew 28:19–20, KJV).

Each of us has a circle of influence that is unique to us. No one else has the same level of contact with the people we know. This also is true in the airline industry. I think of the hundreds of crew members, cabin attendants, gate agents, operations agents, flight dispatchers, aircraft mechanics, and passengers with whom I have had contact.

Early in my career, I asked myself, "How can I share the gospel with so many people?" One method I've used and have found to be helpful is giving out a gospel tract. It's a little brochure that has the complete plan of salvation (including Scripture and additional comments). Because I may have only one contact with that individual, I chose to take that opportunity to give him or her a gospel tract. I tried to give tracts discreetly, respectfully, legally, politely, and graciously. I even checked with the airline for guidelines regarding the distribution of literature. Additionally, I was respectful of anyone who did not wish to receive a tract.

With servers in restaurants or hotel shuttle-van drivers, I would always leave a generous tip and explain that the tract was just an additional way of thanking them for their service.

My wife and I designed a little business card that invites people to read our blog. (You can read more about that on page 59.) On the back, we leave a handwritten note, explaining to our servers that their tip is at the register and thanking them for their great service. On the blog is a tab devoted to our clerks and servers. We have found this to be a quick and effective way to make an impact in situations where we have little time to share much more than this in person.

I used to give tracts to crew members, thanking them for a pleasant trip. I would also thank passengers and would tell them that this material was my *personal* thank-you to them for allowing me to fly them to their destination.

One of the most important things about sharing the gospel through the use of tracts is to have some! There are many well-written gospel tracts. I am happy to be associated with Lifegate, the publishers of "God's Simple Plan of Salvation." To read about their ministry, visit: www.GodsSimplePlan.org.

Even the best of tracts is meaningless if the gospel is not lovingly and faithfully evident in the life of the giver. Live in a way that paves a clear path for the gospel to be received.

ABOUT THE AUTHOR

Joe Henderson, a retired international airline pilot, is lovingly called "Captain Joe" by all who know him well. In his retirement, Joe has joined his wife, Brenda, in her love for writing and frequently contributes to their blog (Petals from the Basket) via "The Captain's Corner," where he intertwines his familiarity with the airline industry with practical biblical lessons.

The Hendersons reside in Indiana, where they are active in their local church and enjoy writing, fishing in neighboring ponds, spending time with family, entertaining, and cheering on the Notre Dame football team!

To visit "The Captain's Corner," go to:
PetalsfromtheBasket.com

Made in the USA
Columbia, SC
08 November 2024

45885060R00037

45885052R00037